TITANIC

TITANIC

Richard A. Boning

Illustrated by

Harry Schaare

The Incredible Series

Barnell Loft, Ltd. Baldwin, New York

To
Peggy E. Ransom

It was 11:40 p.m., the night of April 14, 1912. Five times that day warnings had been received of ice ahead. But no one aboard was concerned. New York was just two days away, and the *Titanic* was unsinkable. Millionaires had flocked from all over the Continent to board her in England just to make this maiden voyage. It was unthinkable that ice could harm this super ship.

In the wireless room Operator John Phillips was a bundle of nerves. For fourteen straight hours he had hammered out messages for wealthy passengers. They all wanted to wire friends at home and on other ships. Then from the operator of the nearby *Californian* came the sixth message of the day.

Like the others, this one warned of ice. Impatiently Phillips placed the message in a basket. He would get to it when there was time. Right now he still had a pile of unsent messages from society figures such as the Strauses, Astors, and Guggenheims. Phillips knew that to ignore wealthy passengers could cost him his job.

Again the warning was repeated. Phillips suddenly lost his temper. "Shut up! Shut up!" he snapped at the operator of the *Californian*. "I'm too busy. You're jamming my signals."

High above the ship in the crow's nest, Lookout Frederick Fleet squinted into the darkness. He thought he saw something. Then out of the night came a spectacle that made Fleet gasp. He could not believe his eyes. Before him loomed a mountain of ice as tall as a seven-story building!

Panic-stricken, Fleet yelled into the phone, "Iceberg ahead!"

For thirty-seven long seconds the lookout wondered if the bridge had received his warning. The iceberg now towered over the ship. As Fleet braced himself for the crash, the *Titanic* veered sharply to port. At the last moment the giant berg floated by. To Fleet it seemed like a close call indeed.

To passengers below there was only a slight jar. A few awakened. "Why has the ship stopped?" one of them asked a steward.

"I don't know, sir," the steward replied. "But I'm sure it's nothing to be concerned about."

To the card players in the smoking room it was not worth interrupting the game for. Someone brought back a piece of ice that had been scraped off the berg. "A souvenir," he chuckled, "for your drinks."

But down in the boiler room it was easy to see that the wound was very serious. As water poured through a gaping hole, the electric doors slammed shut. Two stokers leaped through just in time as a door crashed down behind them. In a matter of seconds a gash 300 feet long had been sliced in the hull of the *Titanic*.

Captain Smith appeared on the bridge, surprised but not alarmed. The giant vessel — a sixth of a mile long — lay quietly in the water, apparently unharmed.

At that moment the builder, Thomas Andrews, approached Smith.

"How is she?" Captain Smith asked him.

Andrews hesitated, and then said simply, "Very bad, I'm afraid."

Captain Smith could feel his mouth go dry. It was difficult for him to comprehend what Andrews was saying. Smith had been told by the owners that the *Titanic* was unsinkable. Now here was the builder telling him the ship was in danger of sinking.

"But the waterproof compartments —" he began to protest.

In a strained voice Andrews explained that the *Titanic* could float with any three of the first compartments flooded. She could float with four of them flooded. But there was no way she could stay up with five compartments full of water.

Captain Smith was dazed by the bad news. It did not seem possible that there could be more. But there was.

"How much time do we have?" he asked Andrews.

"An hour. Maybe two," the builder replied.

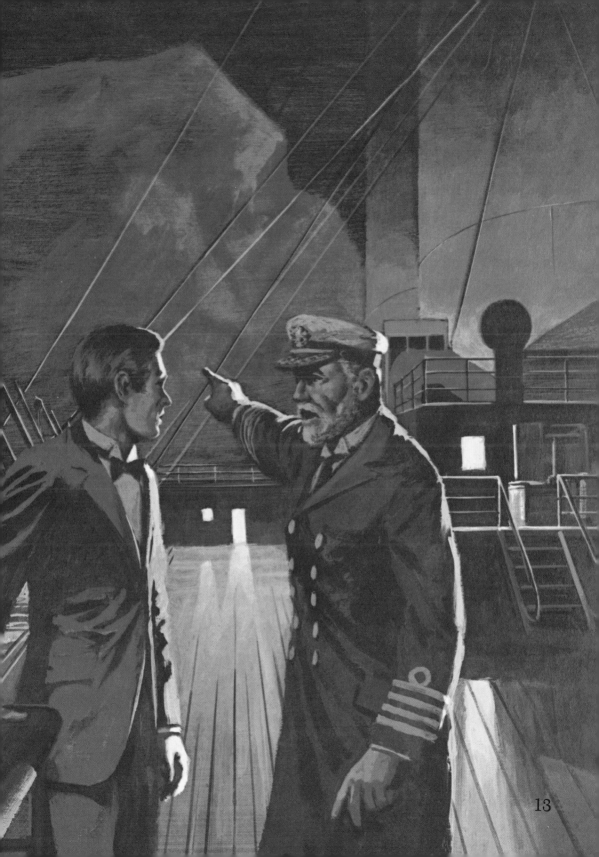

13

Down in the hold the "waterproof" *Titanic* was taking on water at an alarming rate. Green sea water chased the mail clerks to a higher level in the ship's post office. Now it swirled toward the quarters of 700 steerage passengers. Many were immigrants who spoke no English. But they knew that safety lay above. Terrified, they raced to the gate leading to the stairs. To their horror the gate was locked.

In one of the steerage cabins lay fifteen-year-old Katie Gilnagh, now suddenly awake and frightened. Katie had left her home in Ireland and was traveling alone. Yesterday she had tried to go above to the luxurious quarters of the wealthy passengers. But a crew member had refused to open the gate.

Ten miles away Third Officer Charles Groves stared from the deck of the *Californian*. She was a small liner on her way to Boston. She had stopped because of the ice field ahead. Groves saw that the large ship was not moving either. Evidently she had also stopped because of the ice.

15

Captain Smith knew he must act fast. Some crewmen were sent to uncover lifeboats. Others were assigned to man lifeboat stations. As they went about their duties briskly, the disturbance was promptly forgotten by the passengers. The card players and the party-goers had no desire to leave the warmth and cheer of the smoking room for the chill night air.

Like the rest of the world, the passengers knew the *Titanic* was unsinkable. So when Captain Smith went out to oversee the loading of lifeboats, he was stunned by the sight that greeted him.

A small group of passengers was now on deck. Some of them had found a pile of ice that had been scraped off the side of the berg. They were making snowballs and pelting each other!

Stewards hammered on doors, frantically trying to awaken sleeping passengers. Many did not respond. Others complained when they were asked to put on lifebelts.

"It's one of those silly safety drills," said one young man.

The mining king, Benjamin Guggenheim, grumbled that it was all a pack of nonsense. Those passengers who walked out on deck were inclined to agree. There was no sign of a hole in the *Titanic*. She looked as large and secure as ever. There was no way for them to know that water was now pouring into her hold at a rate of thousands of gallons per minute.

Despite the best efforts of the stewards, many passengers returned to bed.

Then Captain Smith recalled a fact about British shipping that made him gasp.

At the time, the number of lifeboats on all British liners was determined by the tonnage of the ship, not the number of people aboard. There were 2207 persons aboard the *Titanic*. There were lifeboats for only 1178.

With heart pounding, Captain Smith knew that if hundreds were not to die help must be summoned from other ships — and soon. Captain Smith opened the door of the wireless shack.

"We've struck an iceberg!" he exclaimed to the operators. "We're going down!"

Phillips and his assistant, Harold Bride, looked at each other, bewildered. The *Titanic* was unsinkable. There must be some mistake.

But blue sparks sputtered as the message flashed out across the Atlantic.

Just ten miles away, Cyril Evans, the operator on the *Californian*, was getting ready for bed. His feelings had been hurt because of the unfriendly reception he had received from the *Titanic*. Even when Officer Groves dropped in, Evans was in no mood to chat.

Groves liked to work the wireless himself. He was just getting the hang of it and found it fun.

"Any calls?" he asked.

"Only the *Titanic*," replied Evans.

Groves put on the headphones and tried to start the machine. It would not respond. He did not know that Evans had let it run down and had not bothered to wind it up.

With anguish Captain Smith realized that sixty precious minutes had gone. He returned to the boat deck. It was now 12:40 a.m., yet the first boats were just being lowered. It had been almost impossible to get women to enter them. In order to reach the lifeboats, it was necessary to step across an open space seventy feet above the water. Many women refused.

22

Some insisted on remaining with their husbands. "We've spent our lives together," said Mrs. Isidor Straus. "Now we will die together." She and her husband calmly strolled about the deck, watching the boats being lowered.

Several times crew members tried to appeal to Mrs. Straus. "At least you must attempt to save your life," they pleaded. Each time she smiled. Each time she refused. Finally she and her husband sat down on deck chairs. No one would ever remember seeing them again.

The Captain sped to the wireless shack.

There he received even more appalling news. Of all the ships that had responded, the closest was the *Carpathia*. It would be several hours before she could appear on the scene. Captain Smith realized that this would be too late — much too late. The *Titanic* was already listing three degrees to starboard.

Now women entered the lifeboats more willingly. Men began trying to sneak in among them. Young Daniel Buckley vaulted into a boat. He covered himself with a shawl. Another young man, a boy in fact, was not so fortunate. Fifth Officer Harold Lowe found him cowering under a seat. The boy pleaded that he would not take up much room, but Lowe drew a gun.

"Please don't shoot him," the passengers begged. But Lowe insisted that the young man get out. After climbing out, the boy lay sobbing on the deck of the *Titanic*.

Down in steerage, passengers required no urging. As the water rose, it drove them up the stairs. Men broke open doors. A long line of steerage passengers wound its way upwards.

Katie Gilnagh knew she must leave too. At the end of the passage, she saw a flight of stairs. There was no time to lose.

As Katie threaded her way upward, she became confused. There were so many halls and passageways. Slowly she made her way from deck to deck. As she neared the boat deck, she wondered why the other steerage passengers had stopped moving. They stood on the stairs, waiting patiently. When Katie got to the top of the stairs, her heart sank. The way was barred by a gate.

"Sorry, miss," said a crewman. "You must use your own deck."

Tears welled up in Katie's eyes. She knew there were no boats on the other decks. Then with a start of terror she saw the last boat about to be lowered!

A steerage passenger, Jim Farrell, roared in anger. "Great God, man!" he bellowed. "Open the gate and let the girl through."

The guard hesitated. Then he stepped aside. Katie found herself running on the open deck. To her surprise she heard the band playing ragtime. If only she could keep from sliding! As she ran toward the boat, it began to disappear over the side.

It was 2 a.m. A strange calm now hung over the vessel. There were no boats left. All the women and children were gone. Captain Smith felt a grim sense of relief. Then he saw a sight that chilled his blood.

Not far away were some bellboys. They were only twelve or thirteen years old. They stood joking and smoking cigarettes. For the first time in the entire voyage there was no adult ordering them around. The boys were having a marvelous time! Captain Smith stared — stunned. Then he sped back to the wireless shack. "For God's sake," he gasped, "tell the *Carpathia* to hurry!"

But the power was almost gone. Only a very weak message could be sent. Water was already at the door of the wireless shack. "You men have done your duty," the Captain announced in a hushed voice. "Now it's every man for himself." Neither man seemed to hear him. They were both intent on coaxing the last spark of life from the wireless set.

Other passengers made final preparations.
Benjamin Guggenheim and his valet had dressed in their tuxedos. They stood by the rail as if awaiting an important social event. "We shall go down like gentlemen," Guggenheim explained.

In the smoking room the famous editor, William T. Stead, sat reading. He looked as if he intended to stay right there until the end.

Shipbuilder Andrews stood in the center of the room. His life jacket lay on the table. He seemed to be staring into the distance. "Aren't you going to make a try for it, sir?" a steward asked. But Andrews gave no sign that he had heard.

Charles Joughin, the ship's baker, decided to prepare himself for a long, cold swim. He drained the contents of a full bottle of gin. Slowly and calmly he adjusted his life jacket.

As the water approached the musicians, Bandmaster Hartley rapped sharply on his violin. The ragtime stopped. There was a pause. Then the beautiful strains of the hymn, "Autumn," floated out over the water. People in the boats listened in awe.

Suddenly, to the dismay of Captain Smith, hundreds of steerage passengers poured out on the decks from below. Everyone had forgotten them. Aghast, he noted that among them were women and children.

The stern of the *Titanic* began to rise from the sea. For a long moment the ship stood straight up. As the boilers ripped loose and fell down through her hull, the noise was deafening. Then, at 2:30 a.m., with a mighty roar the *Titanic* began to slide slowly beneath the surface, her cabin lights still ablaze.

Captain Smith tried to shout instructions through a megaphone. As he did, he shot a glance to the south. There was no sign of the *Carpathia*. He found himself falling.

At first the coldness of the water took his breath away. Beside him a bellboy tried desperately to stay afloat. The Captain reached out for the sinking boy to hold him up. Then everything seemed to grow dim. Strange — the water no longer felt cold. As Smith attempted to support the boy, both were forced farther down. Suddenly the Captain realized that he would never feel anything again.

As the giant ship went under, Second Officer Charles Lightoller found himself dragged down by the suction from a ventilator. Then, just when it appeared he was lost, a blast of hot air blew him to the surface. The shock of the icy water went through him like a current of electricity. No man could live for long at this temperature. He wondered how near the *Carpathia* must be by now. Then he saw an overturned collapsible boat. He began swimming for it and climbed aboard. It was packed with shivering survivors.

Baker Joughin stood on the deck of the *Titanic* as the ship nosed beneath the surface. As the water rushed up to meet him, he stepped out into it like a man leaving an escalator. Calmly, he began swimming for the overturned boat. When he could find no room to climb aboard, he merely clung to the side — cheerful and unaffected by the cold.

Now the people in the boats found that a new sound had replaced the music. It was a horrifying sound, made by hundreds of people sobbing and screaming for help.

At that moment Lightoller discovered another problem that made his temples pound. The collapsible boat was supported only by a giant air bubble. Whenever a swell moved the boat, air escaped from underneath. If something were not done, the boat would soon sink.

"Everybody on his feet," barked Lightoller. He formed the exhausted survivors into columns. Then as the bubble moved from side to side, he ordered the columns to move with it. Thus for the moment the air was trapped below.

Suddenly one of the men pitched forward and rolled off the boat into the freezing water. As he did, another jet of air escaped, and the boat settled even lower.

On board the *Californian* a crewman stepped up to the speaking tube and addressed the Captain. "That strange ship, sir. Now her lights are gone completely. She must have steamed away."

"Very well, carry on," came the sleepy voice of the Captain.

Even though it was 2:30 a.m., lights shone brightly on the *Carpathia*. Anxiously Captain Arthur H. Rostron watched the gauge. Until now thirteen knots had been top speed for his ship. Could he get more out of her? Relays of crewmen shoveled coal furiously into the furnaces.

The old ship seemed to tremble with excitement. The needle on the gauge quivered and moved up — fourteen knots, fifteen knots. Finally the *Carpathia* began to shudder through the water at eighteen knots. At the bow were stationed fourteen lookouts—men with the keenest eyes on the ship. Each had been instructed to watch closely for both icebergs and the *Titanic*. Twisting and dodging, the *Carpathia* wove a dangerous path through the ice fields, firing rockets as she raced ahead at full speed.

Far to the north Lightoller saw a rocket shoot up from the *Carpathia*. Another survivor toppled into the icy water, and the raft settled still lower. The roar of the swimmers had faded. Only an occasional cry could be heard. By 3 a.m. the air was completely still. Numbly Lightoller wondered if the rescue ship would arrive in time.

44

It was a strange-looking scene that greeted the *Carpathia* at dawn. A number of lifeboats were scattered across the water. A group of men appeared to be standing on the water. It was Lightoller and his survivors. There were only twenty of them now. The boat was totally submerged. Still swimming at the side was Baker Joughin, who had been in the water all night. He was still cheerful — still unaffected by the cold.

But nowhere in sight was the mighty liner — the "unsinkable" *Titanic*. Her elegant ballrooms and theaters now lay forever beneath two miles of ocean. As the *Carpathia* picked up survivors, it was clearly too late for the 1503 victims of the tragedy.

Never again would man advertise a ship as unsinkable, nor would ships ignore ice warnings. Never again would third-class passengers be left to drown while first-class passengers were put into lifeboats. But all that lay in the future.

Right now Katie Gilnagh was happy with the present. She was exhausted, but she had survived the night in a lifeboat. She gazed out of the *Carpathia's* open porthole at the sea. It was bright and calm and seemed to stretch out forever.

Her curiosity satisfied, Katie returned to her bunk and yawned. She was looking forward to her new life in America. In moments she was fast asleep.

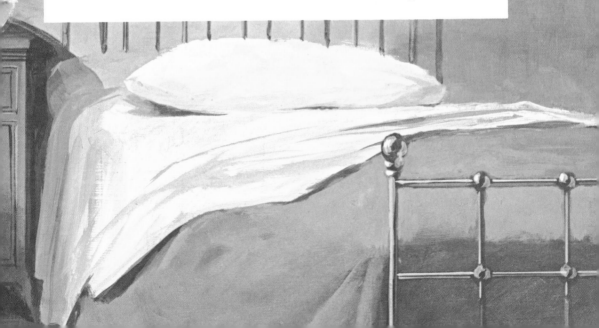